Camino

MW01609465

For Seniors

Prologue

Being a Senior and having done the Camino de Santiago, many things became clear to me. Let me help you.

This book is for Seniors. It is designed to make the Camino more enjoyable and meaningful for you. There are many pitfalls that can be easily avoided. My intent is to help you avoid the many mistakes that I made.

Nearly all the guide books and literature that you will come upon are targeting trekkers that are much younger than you and I. If you are age 50 or more, Sailor take warning and heed some some advise from this senior.

The following chapters will help you regardless of what you are attempting to achieve on the Camino.

You will need to have your Camino Passport. A time saver tip: on the internet, search for friends of the Camino. For a small donation, they will mail you a passport to take with you. A real time saver.

When you return, your passport will look something like this. Many stamps, front and back. Get a stamp everywhere you go. Albergues, cafes, churches, museums, everywhere.

Mine is the most important 'Treasure' I brought back.

Buen Camino

II

Camino de Santiago
For Seniors
Contents

Camino de Santiago
For Seniors
Notes

Camino de Santiago
For Seniors

Before you Go

What to do? What to do? **Make a Checklist!**

Passport? Do you have a passport? Don't laugh, people say of course I have a Passport. Do you remember where it is? Time to pack and they can't find it.

Yesterday is when you should have started physical training. Don't go 'Mall walking' for an hour and say that's it for today. Push yourself harder each and every day. You will be thankful for the punishment you gave yourself during training. You will be pleasantly surprised when one day it becomes apparent to you that you feel better than you have in years. A lot of truth in the saying 'No Pain, No Gain'.

Get a complete Physical right away. I will tell you what happened to me shortly.

Medical insurance? Your medicare is no good in Europe. Get signed up for premium supplemental insurance, the zero co-pay plan 'F' type.

It will cover eighty % of medical costs in Europe. More about that coming up.

It's never to early to start shopping for Air travel tickets. You might get lucky and catch a promotion fare. This is another good reason to do an off-season pilgrimage.

YouTube !!!!! Blogging !!!!! Two ways to get tons of help and information.

It happened to me.

Taking my own advise, I signed up for Plan 'F' supplemental insurance. Let's take it for a spin.

The Dermatologist

I had a tiny little 'thing' on my neck, if I scratched it, it would bleed. Just a tiny little rough place. Stop, I hear what you are saying! Yes, I knew what it was. Dermatologist says yep it's cancerous. She says, what's this?

Here we go. Three on my neck, One on my cheek and one on my back. All were of the mild variety, if there is such a thing. Zero deductible has already paid for itself.

Complete Physical

Okay, let's check the rest of the body. Doc says 'You are a fine specimen for some one your age'. Thanks Doc. Oh one more thing, let's check that Prostate. Uh Oh, definitely enlarged. Gulp!

I always wonder why my doctor wants to have some meaningful conversation while he is fiddling with my prostate. My eyes are crossed and I am hanging on to the exam table for dear life. My replies are always nothing more than groaning noises.

Urologist

Off to the Urology folks. Hmm, biopsy time. What fun. The good news/bad news. No Cancer is good news. The bad news is the prostate has to be reduced. All a success. Yea. Did I mention Zero Deductible?

Get back on the bicycle!

Back to training! How did I lose all the strength I worked so hard for?

Lots of bicycle training. It is paying off. I feel better than I have in years. Too good to last. Early morning, it's rush hour. I'm cruising down a busy four lane street. Only a fool would ride on that street. I'm on the sidewalk where I am safe.   NOT !

Passing a section of businesses. I see one of those big black SUVs coming. A woman staring to her left checking for a traffic opening. Unfortunately for me, there was an opening. She guns it and there is my once smiling face looking at her mouthing some non Christian verbs.

Center Punched would be a good term. Knocked me right out in front of two cars coming fast. Quick thinking by a man driving in the opposite lanes. He saw what happened and swerved into the oncoming lanes to block more cars from hitting me.

In 2006 I was attacked by a Dog and suffered a broken back. The pain was very similar. Anyhow, no broken bones just really sore. It turned out to be my fault for operating a vehicle on the sidewalk.

The point is, 5 hours in the Trauma center came to over $26,000. **Zero deductible!**Back to training! No more busy streets. My routine was Bicycle early in the day, Four miles minimum. Walk with pack, four miles minimum. During really hot weather, yes, mall walking for two hours. Another bicycle ride.

Monday, Wednesday and Friday off to the YWCA. Yes YWCA, it's close by and it's inexpensive.

Camino de Santiago
For Seniors

WHY ?

The most common reason is naturally religious. Many want to strengthen their connection with God. There will be many opportunities to do that. Take some time and visit the many churches and cathedrals along the 'Way'. Many will be very moving.

For myself, long personal conversations with God has lifted me to more Peace than I could have even hoped for. Places such as the Cruz de Ferro actually took my breath away. There was a spirit there for me that 'Rocked My World' so to speak. Was there actually a spirit there? For myself, there was because I wanted it to be there. Simple really. To other Pilgrims, it might be just a huge pile of stones that have been carried there from all over the world.

Some do the Camino just for adventure. Nothing wrong with that either. Many find that the simple act of a long trek will end up walking with God. If not, the Camino will give you a look at some of the most beautiful places on Earth.

Some make the pilgrimage for forgiveness. Many will find just that. Many College students walk the Camino to have it on their Resume. It carries a lot of weight in many countries. Think about it, if you were wanting to hire a new employee and you have two candidates that are equal with the only exception being one had walked the Camino de Santiago, which would you hire?

On many segments of the Camino, there are 'Optional' routes. The easier path will take you along the country roads or secondary highways. Many areas will have concrete barriers between trekkers and the highway. It is safe.

As your stamina improves, you will opt for the optional paths that take you away from any road. A walk through a forest for an hour or two will be a special time to clear your mind. It is an amazing thing. You will find that you have terribly cluttered your mind with thoughts of Radio, TV, autos and all sorts of 'Forced' thoughts.

Even if you are walking with a 'partner' there should be times when you walk alone. Try it. Agree to meet at a specific Albergue and walk alone for a segment, especially if it is through the countryside or a forest. You will love it, just you and your God.

Do not forget to carry a stone in your pocket from your home. When you walk in those quiet areas, rub the stone and put your life burdens on that stone.

Many of us carry sins that we have a hard time believing can be forgiven. Load that stone with those sins. I did. When you arrive at the Cruz de Ferro, I truly hope the spirit of God grabs your soul like it did mine. By the time I reached the Cross of Iron, I had rehearsed what I was going to say hundreds of times, yet when I arrived, I couldn't speak. I could barely stand. I finally got it done, but I was there a long time.

The Author at The Cruz de Ferro

This may sound strange, but I could feel the spirit going from the ground up through my feet and my life has changed forever.

I had an Epiphany if you will while I was there. From the time I was a child, I was taught the 'Law' from the Old Testament and Grace from the New Testament. What I realized there at the Cruz de Ferro was that the Bible is great reading and it serves to keep you on track, the bottom line is simple........... It's me and God. If God is Happy with me, I am Happy with God. It is just that simple. I left the Cruz de Ferro in complete and total Peace !

I had a similar experience in the Cathedral at Santiago.

I sincerely hope you have a similar experience.

Later in my travel I met a younger man from Germany. During our conversation, I related my experience and I asked if he had a reaction there. He said he did and then told me about his partner for that day.

He said he had been trekking alone (He started at his home in Germany, wow). He said that morning as he was preparing to leave the Albergue, a gentleman asked if he could tag along. Sure. He said they got along great pace wise and few words. Later in the day, they were approaching the hill top and the man asked if he felt it. He said yes. A few more paces and the Cruz was in view. About that time, he heard a thud behind him. The man was on his face. He suffered a heart attack. The man survived but he would have to complete his Camino another time.

I was somewhere near Santiago and I met a man from Ireland he was a really nice man. I asked if he would like to walk the last kilometers with me and he said no. he did not want to see the Cathedral until next year. He said he had taken the bus from Lugo and got off just before we met. He said he did one portion of the Camino every year for a week on his vacation. This was his 5th year. The following year he would complete the pilgrimage by trekking from Lugo to Santiago. We said goodbye and he turned off to go to the Airport at Santiago. Truly a good man.

Take your time. If you are a retiree (pensioner in Europe), why be in a hurry. Smell the Roses pilgrim.

Camino de Santiago
For Seniors

When?

Choosing the time of year is important. Some like hot weather, some like colder weather. I selected mid September as the starting time for several reasons.

A look at the globe will help you with your understanding of weather patterns in Spain. Most people think that Spain is much further South than it actually is. A glance at the globe view will show you that Madrid and New York City are very close to being at the same Latitude. Surprised? I was. Considering that the Camino de Santiago is well North of Madrid, the Latitude would be closer to that of Upstate New York. That means, moderate summers and cold winters.

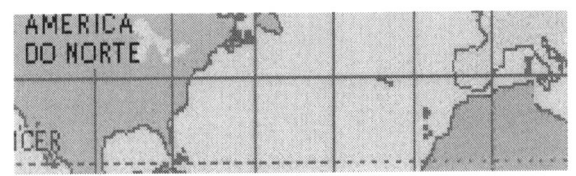

First, most of the guide book information seemed to indicate that autumn has the most even weather patterns. My experience confirmed that. The first foul weather I encountered was the first day I arrived in Santiago. Trust me, trekking in mud is no fun at all.

Secondly, most school kids are not on the Camino. If you are trekking at a sensible pace on a Natural Path and are deep in meditation, there is nothing more disturbing than twenty students that consider the Camino a Race and are loudly singing songs. Yes, it will happen and it will happen much more often in the summer. Hmm, that sounds mean. I love my grand kids more than life itself, but when it's time, I also enjoy sending them home.

Thirdly, The Camino de Santiago is growing in popularity at an incredible rate. In the Autumn, finding a Albergue is MUCH easier. Sleeping on a floor is not an acceptable rest area for seniors.

In the event this might happen to me, I carried a self-inflating sleeping mat. I never used it. Just more weight to carry.

Fourth, Even if you are making the Pilgrimage with a partner, there will be times when you will want to trek in solitude for some time. The purest times are when you are on a 'Natural' path through pasture land or mountains or Forest land.

These times you will come to cherish. It is amazing how quickly this will happen. Just you and your God out for a walk and having the best conversation ever. Get rid of all that trash in your brain. It was amazing to me when I realized all the clutter that was in my head. Today, I make a conscious effort to purge the trash from my mind. It's a good thing I learned. No TV, No radio, just do it. You will love it.

Camino de Santiago
For Seniors

Where ?

Most guide books start in St Jean Pied de Port France. Oh Boy, start right off in the Pyrenees Mountains and the first leg takes you twenty five kilometers up the mountains to Roncesvalles Spain. Arguably the toughest leg of the Pilgrimage and you have another 800 Km to go. It is Very steep and has ruined a lot of pilgrimages.

This choice is Critical!

Take a lot of time and think about it. There are numerous places that you can start from. You are a Senior, not a "track Star'. A truly smart choice would be to start your pilgrimage at some point other than the beginning.

If you are successful, you can bus back to another starting point.

A starting point in the plains could be a good option. Get those legs tuned up for the mountains.

You can start as far along the Camino as Sarria and still receive your Compostela (certificate of pilgrimage). I do not recommend that, because a lot of pilgrims start there. The 'Way' will be busy from Sarria to Santiago. The serene experience will be tarnished. I would much rather walk 100km on the plains. The last 100km might have you craving solitude, especially if you have experienced true quiet earlier on the Camino.

A smart choice would be to start at Ponferrada for several reasons. The first would be travel to Ponferrada. It is quite easy from Madrid. Chamartin train station is only a short distance from the Airport. Catch a train to Ponferrada. The train is amazing. Stay an extra day in Ponferrada and tour the Knights templar Castle. Jet Lag is tough.

Secondly, you will still have plenty of natural paths to enjoy. You will test your conditioning on your climb to O'Cebreiro where you cross into Galicia.

Ponferrada to Santiago is roughly 25% of the Camino. If you complete that and want more, Bus or train back as far as you want and start back again from your new location. It is a smart choice.

Don't try to be a hero. You will ruin your experience.

A second leg might be St Jean France to Puente La Riena for example. The options are numerous. Buses and trains are cheap, clean, fast and frequent.

One last time, your choices of how far you go can make or break your experience.

The Author at La Portella de Valcarce. 580 km done, 190km to go. You can do it.

Camino de Santiago
For Seniors

Travel

One of the few places we seniors get a break. Air travel and train travel in Spain is cheaper for us. If you are traveling from the United States, you have multiple choices of how to get to Europe. Check ALL the sites and airlines themselves for bargains.

You need to consider this, you are a senior and that usually means that you are not burdened with a 'Time table'. Use that information and do not Book 'Round Trip'. One way is more expensive, but it is worth it. If you are on a schedule, it can only hurt your experience. You can easily find yourself needing more 'Rest' days than you anticipated.

For example, say you have booked for a round trip time of one month. You have three days left before you return and you are four or more days from Santiago. Call the Airline? You will lose one arm and one leg so to speak. What if you have been there for a week and get injured? Same thing.

I recommend Madrid to be your first destination. You will see a lot of Pilgrims there. It is also connected with the Rail system. Paris is good also, but it will take longer to get to your starting point.

My choice was to fly American Airlines. When my ticket arrived, I found that I was actually flying on Iberia Airlines from Miami to Madrid. They are THE BEST. A brand new Airbus with Spanish 'Barbie' doll hostesses. Fabulous food and you can start your training on Tempranilo wine from Spain. Really tasty.

The earlier you book, the better. I have watched the airfares and they do not drop dramatically in the last few days. They may drop with a couple hours left before the flight, so it is your call.

Booking rail a ticket is easy. You can do it on the internet before you leave if you worry about connections as a lot of us do.

When you get to Spain, you will find bilingual people every where. I crammed with a free Spanish course on YouTube. Through my tour of Spain, I found my most common phrase was unpoco espanol (I speak a little Spanish), yet I got by. If you refer to yourself as a 'Crazy American', you will be readily accepted with a big smile and locals will go out of their way to help you. It worked every time for this pilgrim.

One thing became readily apparent, Never, ever bring up the topic of the European Union. The people of Spain are the calmest, most 'Laid Back' people in the world, but mention the words European Union and passions will boil. I was quite surprised that they were not the first to withdraw.

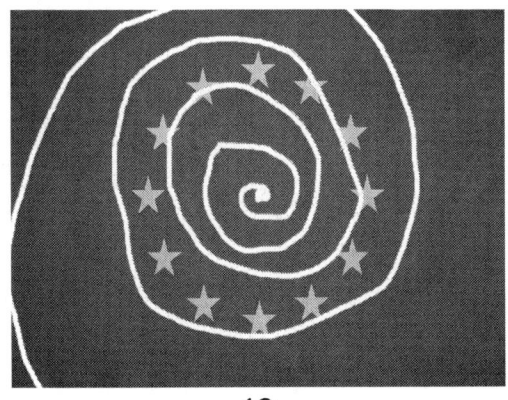

19

We saw many European Union signs disfigured like this. Most with the Helix, others with a red X.

I made the mistake of asking what that was all about. The feeling was that during the money conversion to Euros, the Spanish did not fare well at all.

Inflation is another point. Trust me, they will tell you about their grievances in detail.

Camino de Santiago
For Seniors

Euros

How many Euros should I take in cash? The amount you carry in cash is variable on the trekking style you bring. If you are planning on staying in Albergues exclusively, the amount of cash you need will be greatly reduced. Staying in the small hotels or Hostels, more cash.

Let me say right here, there is virtually zero crime in Spain. You can stroll around in a very poorly lit town at midnight and feel perfectly safe. It is amazing. During the six weeks I was there, the only thing I had stolen was a bar of soap I left in a shower. I realized it was missing about three hours after I showered. The lost & found at the Albergue had about six bars, but not mine. Made me wonder if whoever got my soap had any idea of places that it had been. Ha.

In six weeks, I did not hear of a single problem with theft or any other crime. It will become quickly apparent how safe it is. About 60 % of the pilgrims are female and many are walking alone.

Credit Cards. Check with your credit card provider about using your credit card in Europe. DO NOT take 'Oh Sure' for an answer. Ask about additional charges that may apply to each usage of your card. The average Telephone contact does not know and you may get wrong answers. Go to your bank and talk to an officer. Will they wire you Euros in case of emergency?

Find a credit card provider that is EURO friendly. It is best to have cards from more than one provider.

I carried two, one VISA and one MASTER CARD plus a debit card from my bank. You may get somewhere that one card may not work but another will. It happened to me several times.

It is best to have a waterproof pouch that you can wear to the showers for your money and your passport. Many choices available on ebay.

Speaking of Passports, make a photocopy of yours and place it in your wallet. Should your passport become lost for any reason, a replacement will be many times easier with the photocopy.

Spend a few minutes and calculate a daily budget, multiply that by the number of weeks you are comfortable with and you will have a good idea of how much cash to have on hand.

ATM, magical letters. The same as in the U.S.   Almost every bank has one outside. They are found in businesses also, like Mercados (Grocery stores). I did have problems where an ATM did not accept a credit card but the same ATM would accept another of my cards.

Camino de Santiago
For Seniors
WHAT TO TAKE ?

The correct answer is 10 % of what you will end up taking. It seems like no one will listen to this point. I wish I could meet each of you at your starting point and confiscate 90 % of your non essentials and mail them on to Santiago. Many people do just that. Search the internet and you can locate businesses in Santiago that you can ship your baggage to. For a reasonable fee, they will store your items for you until you arrive to pick them up.

If you find your backpack is still too heavy, each albergue can assist you in having that heavy pack forwarded to the next albergue of your choice. This can be a true blessing.

Do not buy a giant backpack. You will just fill it and it will cripple you. Think small! When shopping for a pack, Try every back pack available. Find the one that fits you, especially your hips. Comfort is CRITICAL!

The truth is, Guys can get by just fine with:

three T-shirts

three pair of underwear

four pair of socks

one pair of gloves

one hat

One scarf

SPF30 UV protection (SMALL!)

one pair of hiking boots Water Proof and as light as possible. Do some serious shopping here. Wear them during all training. You do NOT want to start your trek with new boots. You can if you enjoy pain.

One pair of walking shoes for when you are in the plains. Again, as light as you can find.

Get the BEST Gel shoe inserts that you can find.

One Towel Those small micro fiber towels are great and they can be used for cooling also.

Rain suit also light weight like Frog Togs

Fleece jacket that can be used under the rain gear.

One pair of jeans (well broken in)

One pair of lightweight pants w/detachable leggings.

two pair of lightweight shorts.

One Roll Toilet Paper (some trekkers forget this and are sorry later)

Small 1st aid kit make sure you have liquid bandage. It's great for blisters. When you get the first warning that you might have a blister starting, STOP and use one of your bandages right away.

Foot care is the #1 priority for you. A serious massage every night is amazing.

2"x2" bandage pads. Only a couple, you can get more at any Pharmacia

4"X4" Bandage pads

Hygiene kit. Keep it simple. Soap, tooth paste, powder and deodorant.   If you must shave, get a product called "Miracle Shave". A couple drops and your set for a good shave.

Find the most light weight sleeping Bag.

A Journal to write in. Just a few words every day about where you have been, people you meet, just about your experiences.

In years to come, It will be a prized possession for you or your descendants. I have mine in a safe that comes out when my grand children are visiting. They all want it when I leave this earth. I am thinking they may have to publish it so all can have a copy. I have included a few journal pages for you at the end.

A sleeping bag liner is great if you have insect concerns. I never encountered 'Bed Bugs' but I had heard others say they did. I had heard the stories about pilgrims having to sleep on concrete floors because, "There was No room in the Inn", for this reason, I carried a self inflating sleeping mat. I never used it.

On a couple of occasions, the Albergue of choice was full. I always found another or an inexpensive hotel near by.

Ladies, follow the male list and adapt to your own needs. Most women I talked with said two sports bras were plenty.

Have to have makeup? It's all about weight. Save yourself.

How about a Tent? NOT for seniors.

If you are really tough, take the lightest weight tent you can find and then you need a ground mat.

See above mentioned sleeping mat. Like eating Chocolate, the pounds keep coming. I am not opposed to sleeping out on occasion., but at the end of the day, you will be ready for a shower.

Noise is a problem in an Alberque. At first, I had a hard time with the noise. Snoring is the worst, followed by the bed turner on a squeaky bunk bed. Yes, the occasional loud fart followed by numerous giggles. It's all part of the Albergue music. Soon, it dawned on me.

I had an ipod loaded with a lot of "Elevator" music. My plan was to use it during contemplation times on the Camino. I do not think I used the ipod once on the Camino. I did however use it almost every night. No more snoring snoring music.

It's just more weight to carry. Your choice......

Remember, Spain is a civilized country. You can get anything you need along the 'Way'. Even the smallest towns have a Pharmacia. In Spain, you can purchase many items that are prescription items in the United States.

For example, at one point I had a serious back issue and a doctor friend in the U.S. suggested I find a Pharmacia and purchase Voltarin which is a NSAID cream that is amazing. It is an 'Over the Counter' drug in Europe.

Now, I am sure you are thinking that is not enough gear. Do you want more? Every Albergue for the first few legs of the Pilgrimage will have many items for you that were left behind by other perigrinos that struggled mightily to carry over the Pyrenees. Most will be free or nearly free. Go Light my friend, you will thank me.

Okay, now you are thinking about the end of your pilgrimage. What to wear then? You don't want to look like a bum, right? Santiago is a CITY. They have every level of shopping from Walmart type to Saks 5th Ave. Go ahead, splurge on something new to blend in with the Auto Trekkers.

You can then follow the time honored tradition of taking your pilgrimage clothes to Finesterre and burn them in the rocks there. You will find plenty of burn sites, it is a tradition that has gone on for centuries.

A simple light weight pack will make for a happy pilgrim. Easily the MOST important advice I can give you.

Almost all pilgrims will be carrying half the weight at the end of the trek than they were carrying at the beginning. Wisdom is a slow process.

Assuming you are training every day for months, load up your pack, take a couple liters of water and wear your pack every day. You will soon learn about weight and you will learn if you have 'Pinch Points' on your pack. If you get chafing on a training walk, you will have bleeding after 100km.

Think LIGHTWEIGHT!

Buen Camino

What to take

Notes

What to take

Notes

Camino de Santiag
For Seniors

The Guide Books

A guide book is essential to help you have a great Camino. I researched many of them before I chose **'A Pilgrim's Guide to the Camino de Santiago' by John Brierley**. It is readily available many places. I found bargain prices on **ebay**.

A great feature is a daily reading as you walk.

Some of the features I used the most were the daily albergue listings and locations. Where is the next drinking font? And most important was the route and alternate routes.

For example, the very first segment from St Jean' France to Roncesvalles Spain. The Pyrenees mountains can be avoided in the event of bad weather.

Keep in mind there are dangers. If you start up the mountain path, short of turning around, you are committed and you can face weather changes. The guide book will show there is an alternate route that follows a country road. Just sayin'.

As you walk, you can read about the historical information about the places you are passing. Slow down and enjoy the Camino. If you are getting really tired and you find a nice albergue, take a rest day and spend an extra night. Your body and your mind will be really happy.

Easily, the best feature of his guide is the maps. There are 33 sectional maps, one or more for each segment of the Pilgrimage.

The maps are generally for 20 to 30 km of the trek. There are additional maps for the more populated areas to keep you on the 'Way'.

Most importantly each segment will list all of the rest areas, Albergues, hotels etc. A study of your planned trek for a day, may not work out. DO NOT punish yourself. Pick an albergue short of your planned destination and stop for the night. Every albergue is clearly marked on the maps.

Each map will also show alternate routes and they are color coded from easy to difficult. If you choose to avoid a difficult elevation change you can elect to do so.

Each segment also has a map that shows elevation changes.

Camino de Santiago
For Seniors

Albergues

What is an Albergue? A place to rest. No frills, just a place to rest, meet fellow pilgrims and get the road grime off. Some have very basic meals. My experience proved that they were very clean also.

Remember, you are in Europe, so if you are in a large Albergue, you may be and probably will be confronted with the opposite sex in the showers. The pilgrims from France are very casual about nudity. You will certainly see both sexes with the most basic garments in the Albergues. It is simply a way of life on the Camino.

Should you option for more privacy, most villages will have small hotels that are quite inexpensive. I found this to be a nice break on a couple of occasions.

Albergues

Monastery and or Convent.

I like these. Usually large and a common room for all, often in a structure that may be a thousand or more years old. A must do at least part of your pilgrimage.

Not the best if you are a light sleeper. You will hear everything in there. Somethings are not pleasant when you are tired. I thought I was a light sleeper, but after 30km of trekking you will sleep like never before.

If you like to "sleep-in" forget the big Albergues. Pilgrims are stirring for the days trek at 4am. Some earlier. Pilgrims are polite folks, but no matter how cautious they are about noise, They will wake you. Within minutes, everyone is on the move.

Most will have a basic meal. Be prepared to have a lot of soup and cheese. It is good food, just basic.

Private

More expensive, but usually in a more modern building. Most will have smaller rooms that will have an average of six beds.

Some are very small. You will be more like a house guest. Meals can be terrific or non-existent.

Municipal

These are normally owned and operated by a village or city. I would say closer to a hostel. Facilities and quality will vary. Some of the pilgrims thought they were great, others gave the question the thumbs down. Check it out, you don't have to stay there if there are other choices available.

Chain type

I call them Chain type, others call them 'Network'. Rather like a poor man's Best Western. They are all owned and operated by a company. They are usually above average and are moderately priced.

Most Albergues are closed until 2pm. Many of your fellow pilgrims want to be there when the doors open to get first choice of where to sleep. This is the main reason why perigrinos are on the Camino at 4am. I have done it, but then I wonder what I missed in the dark.

There is a courtesy rule at all Albergues. If you arrive before opening, Backpacks are placed in a row at the front door in the order you arrived. Then you can find a shade tree to have a siesta.

Generally speaking, most Albergues that do not provide a basic meal, do provide facilities to prepare your own meal. They will have pots and pans, dishes and knives/forks. This being said, it might be a smart idea to carry one or more dehydrated meals with you. They are amazingly tasty.

Albergue at LaFaba

THIS IS IMPORTANT ! Always check your guide book for Albergues along your route. You might get to an Albergue you selected and find it is full or you just do not like it. The next Albergue may be 20km further. Save yourself! If you have trekked 30 km already, it is best to back track 2 km than it is to keep going another 20km. Please believe me, the latter can be a killer. I know, because it IS a mistake I made.

Bottom line. At the end of the day, you will not care what type of Albergue you have found. It is a place to have a shower and a place to meet new people. Most importantly, sleep.

Buen Camino

Camino de Santiago
For Seniors

Trekking

The actual walk. Punishment or Pleasure, it's your call. If you have a partner, you are going to have to talk it over. If one is a faster trekker than the other, it can be miserable for both of you. The Camino is SAFE! Let the faster trekker go on ahead. Talk about where the intended stop will be. The faster trekker can secure the sleeping arrangements for both of you. You will be happier. Both of you.

Walking stick, everyone will have one. Classic wood or modern collapsible aluminum. I used the latter. Some ergonomics expert determined that they will make your pilgrimage 30% easier. How do you prove that? I tend to believe it. I tried with and without. It just felt strange without a walking stick.

One of the worst parts of trekking is the lack of sanitary facilities. In the plains, you will see numerous pilgrims, Off roading if you will.

In the hills, you may crest a hill to find someone doing a necessary task. Is it right or wrong? All to often, there is no choice.

Most pilgrims are considerate of others and bury waste. Others are not. If you see a nice rock to sit and rest on, check the backside. You are warned, enough of that.

Your Feet! Change socks in the middle of the days trek. Happy Feet for sure. Feel something starting to irritate a foot, STOP and fix it before the nasty blister takes charge.

Going to be walking an paved paths for a ways, put on walking shoes. Give your boots and your feet a break. Happy Feet! See a nice looking stream? Put those bare feet in the ice cold water. SOOOO good. Put yourself in also if you dare.

Camino de Santiago
For Seniors
Along the WAY

If you start in **St. Jean Pied De Port, France,** Your history lesson begins with your very first step.

Your walk begins as you pass through the Porte St Jacques that was built by the Romans. Thought provoking to be aware of the construction at the time of Christ.

Then it's one foot after the other until you reach the Portico of Glory at Santiago de Compostela. Buen Camino.

This is the WAY

Just follow the Arrows. It's that simple.

Bail Out ! The trek to Roncesvalles is arguably the toughest (if you use the preferred route) of the entire Camino Frances. If you feel you can't make it over the top to Roncesvalles, short of spending the night on the ground, you have ONE option.

The Alberque Orisson that is a little less than half way up the mountain. As far as alberques go, this is as close to a 5 star alberque as you can get. Be fore warned, it fills fast. Many realize their limitations and phone in a reservation.

Something to think about. Ph 0559-491 303

Drinking Font

A typical drinking font. Every time you come upon one (they will be marked in your guide book) Dump the the old water and get fresh spring water that is COLD and sweet. I never heard of anyone having a health issue with water. A few days from now, you will come upon a font that dives you excellent Red Wine. Makes for a smiling pilgrim.

Roncesvalles, Espana. The first village you will come to after crossing into Spain. Your first taste of a large albergue will test you. You will be so tired from climbing the Pyrenees that you will sleep like a baby. Much history happened there. The end of Charlemagne's rear guard were decimated there. You can view their remains in a well.

Albergue Roncesvalles

Still a bit further.

Pamplona A couple of days away from Roncesvalles and a gradual descent all the way. Rather rewarding after the Pyrenees. Enjoy Pamplona and join Hemingway for tapas and Mahou beer. Run with the bulls if you are there at the right time.

Roman Aqueduct near Pamplona

The Roman Aqueducts. I have always had interests in engineering, seeing the aqueducts was amazing to me. How could they determine grading of these canals so the water could barely move in the right direction. Too much slope and the water would not reach the desired destination. Too little slope, no flow at all. Consider that many of these structures were built before the birth of Christ and they are still standing. They had true craftsmen in that era.

Thank you Lord for making the walk to Larasoana mostly downhill. My legs had been saying unkind things to me.

Off to **Pamplona**, to meet Hemingway and run with the bulls. A couple of climbs along the way, but trivial compared to the Pyrenees.

Alto del Perdon The Mountain top made famous by Emilio Esteves and Martin Sheen. A great place for a 'Selfie'. It is a long trek to the top. You will be ready to stop and rest. Many photos taken here. The whining sounds of the wind turbines was not to my liking.

The author at Alto del Perdon

   It always feels so good to get the pack off for 10 minutes.

   This would be a perfect time to mention that in Spain, a STOP sign says, STOP.   In Mexico, a Stop sign says, ALTO.   In Spain, Alto is a summit. Trivia......

Puenta La Reina I could spend a whole day there marveling at the Roman engineering that built the bridge there. This was from the time of Christ or before. Amazing.

   Several Albergues there that are really good. Having choices is a good thing.

They try harder to be the most appealing.

Puenta La Reina

Torres Del Rio, I mention this location not because of the crazy man in the movie but because of the Alto Del Poyo that comes a little less than 3km after Torres Del Rio. Don't celebrate too much at the top. The decent is one of the steepest on the Camino. **More injuries are sustained on downhill portions than uphill sections. Be Warned.**

Logrono. Some say they have the best Tapas in all of Spain. I should mention that other cities make the same claim. Two large Tapas (your choice, they will provide menus) and two Estrella Galacias, Four Euros. It's a full meal. MMMM Tapas, like free apps in the U.S. Only four times bigger and four times better. Another warning, three or more Estrella Galacia beers and you may need to call the next day, a rest day. Not a bad idea.

More trivia, no need to fret about what beer to have. Most taverns and tapas places serve only one flavor. Either Estrella Galacia or Mahou.

Unfortunately, I have yet to find Mahou Beer in the U.S. I have found all the great Rioja wines and that is a good thing. I guess I should say that I am Lutheran, so I am preeminently qualified to say that Mahou gets the nod.

Navarette All of the small villages of Spain have large churches or Cathedrals. You will soon notice that the largest structure in every village will be the church. Many you will pass without a second glance. Do not miss the church in Navarette. Did you ever wonder what happened to the Gold that was plundered by the Spaniards from the Inca Indians of Central America. You will soon see.

It's all Gold

For one Euro, you can turn on the Lights for a few minutes. Well worth it.

Burgos to Astorga, The Plains. Many beautiful sights and history in Burgos. Most importantly, the beginning of the Plains. Weather permitting, easy trekking for a number of days. A great time for a long conversation with your God.

Warning check your guide book for Drinking fonts and albergues. It can be a long way from one to the next once in the plains.. It is much flatter terrain, so carry an extra water supply. Storms can appear quickly and with a storm comes MUD!

Mud is no fun at all. Spending an extra 'Rest Day' at an Albergue will make for a happy peregrino.

Cruz de Ferro. Not long after Astorga, you begin the climb to The Cross of Iron. It is best to spend the night in the Rabanal Albergue before the climb to the Cruz de Ferro for two reasons. The first is to be fresh for the climb. It is not too steep, but it is non stop. The second reason is it will allow you more time at the Cross.

On the way to the top, carry your stone in your hand and load it with your life burdens. I hope it has the same effect on you as it did me. I was speechless for a long time. It went straight into my soul. I was there quite some time before I could say the words I had rehearsed a hundred times. I WAS a different person when I left.

The Author at Cruz de Fero

I could barely stand

Ponferrada The start of the last 25% of the Camino. A great place to start your Pilgrimage if you want to do it in segments. Direct rail from Madrid is great and cheap. The rail station (Estacion de tren) is less than one kilometer from the Camino. Plenty of places to spend the night to rest before you start.

The Knights Templar Castle is right in town and the Way, passes along side. I toured the Castle and it was okay, but not particularly exciting to me.

Knight's Templar Castle at Ponferadda

Villafranca to O'Cebreiro is hard. No getting around it. There are two climbs. The first you will see when you leave Villafranca. It is the steeper of the climbs, but it is easier of the two. The second climb is from Herrerias to O'Cebreiro. Be careful on this one. Large rocks that you climb/navigate and seem to go on forever.

Half way up this climb is the albergue at LaFaba. Give your body a break and stay there. The albergue is well run and one of the best I stayed at. It is about 100 meters off to the right. Watch for the sign.

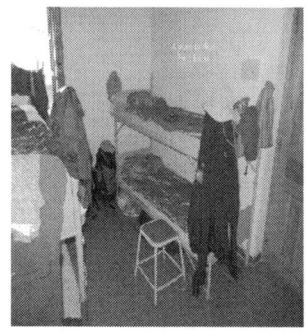

Albergue at LaFaba

O'Cebreiro Welcome to Galicia! The toughest of the climbs are behind you.

For myself, the next segments were the best. Lots of history and spiritual happenings.

A fun thing is coming. About 5km beyond Estella is the Hotel Irache. The fun thing is that they have a drinking font. The very best of the drinking fonts. One tap for great spring water, another tap for Red Wine. All FREE! There are two problems. One is that there is a limited supply so it goes quickly. The second is that all pilgrims know about it.

There are two solutions, if you are at an albergue in Estella, Leave early. The second solution is to stay at the hotel Irache. Give yourself a treat. It's not expensive. That will give you the first opportunity for the free wine before the pilgrims begin arriving from Estella. Just sayin'.

On to the **Cruz de Ferro**. Easily my most moving experience.

Sarria a small city actually. Everything is available here. Albergues to multi Star hotels. This is the beginning of the final trek to Santiago.

It is more than 100 kilometers to Santiago. This means that anyone starting in Sarria is eligible to receive a compostela, the certificate for completion of a pilgrimage.

100 kilometers to go!

Being honest, I will tell you that the last portion of the Pilgrimage was my least favorite. From Sarria to Santiago, the number of Pilgrims seemed to triple. Lots of groups, bicycles and vacationers, not true pilgrims. A completely different atmosphere.

With the increased number of trekkers, comes increased competition for a bed in an albergue. Plan for early stops.

My attitude was on the decline until......

First sighting of the Cathedral at Santiago

My spirit was restored seeing the Cathedral in the distance.

Santiago Oh my, The crypt of St James.

The swinging of the Poterofumeiro. All of it was very Moving. It happened that the Royal family from Portugal was there when I had my first visit. The Mass was amazing.

One disappointment. They will no-longer allow Pilgrims to touch the statue of St James.

I hope you will allow time to explore Santiago. There is much to see.

On a sad note, I walked by a busy Bus Stop numerous times and I couldn't help but notice almost every teenage girl was smoking cigarettes. There were lots of them. Going by a store, I noticed cigarettes for sale. 6-8 Euros per pack! Just sad. How could they afford that?

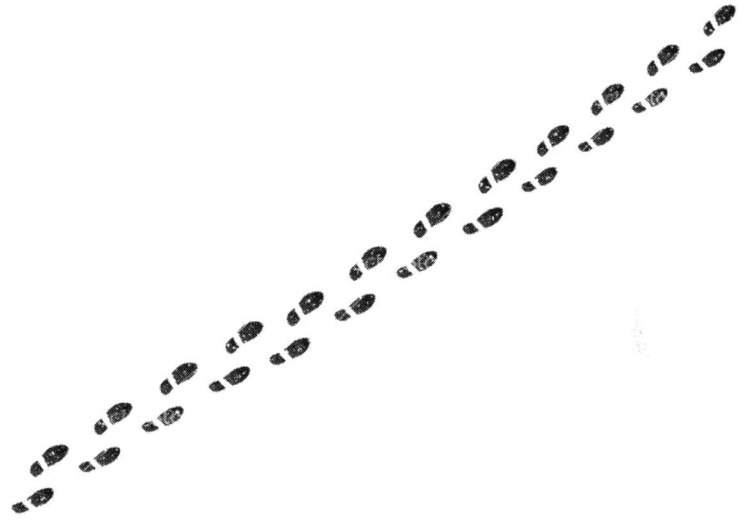

Just one step after another.

Camino de Santiago
For Seniors

Emergency 112
Not 911

Call 112 then be patient. I watched this Ambulancia (Ambulance) take ten minutes to make this turn. Three medics and about twenty back and forth moves. Remember, these streets were made centuries before autos.

Albergue Phone contact

Note: The Albergues listed below are in order from St Jean France to Santiago Spain. Buen Camino.

Hunto, France	0559-371 117
Orisson, France	0559-491 303
Roncesvalles, Spain	948 760 000
Zubiri	609 736 420
Larrasoana	605 505 489
Trinidad de Arre	948 332 941
Pamplona-Ibarrola	948 223 332
Pamplona-Jesus y Maria	948 222 644
Uterga	948 344 598
Puenta la Reina- Monastery	948 340 050
Puenta la Reina-Jakue	948 341 017
Puenta la Reina- Santiago Apostol	948 340 220
Cirauqui Plaza	678 635 208
Lorca	948 541 162
Estella-Hospital de Perigrinos	948 550 200
Estella-San Miguel	615 451 909
Estella-San Cipriano	948 554 311
Villamayor-Santa Cruz	
Villamayor-Hogar	948 537 136
Villamayor-Montedeio	948 551 521
Los Arcos-la Fuente	948 640 791
Los Arcos-Casa Abuela	948 640 250
Los Arcos-Isaac Santiago	948 441 091
Torres del Rio-Casa Mariela	948 648 251
Torres del Rio-La Pata	948 378 457
Torres del Rio-Casa Mari	948 648 409
Rio Cornava	948 090 002

Viana Iglesia de Santa Maria-	
Santa Maria	948 645 037
Viana Iglesia de Santa Maria-	
Andres Munoz	948 645 530
Logrono-Albergue	941 248 686
" - Entresvenos	941 271 334
" - Rioja	941 272 329
" - Puerta	941 700 832
Navarette-Albergue	941 440 732
" - Albergue Navarette	
	630 982 928
" - El Centro	941 441 180
Cruce Opcion	670 053 229
Cruce Opcion Saturnino	941 441 899
Najera-Puerta de Najera	941 362 317
Najera-Alberone	674 246 826
Najera-Sancho III	941 361 138
Najera-Calle Mayor	941 360 407
Azofra Centro	941 379 220
" " - Hostel	607 383 811
Ciruena-Virgen Candelas	687877 891
" -Casa Victoria	941 426 105
Santo Domingode La Calzada	941 343 390
" " -Convent	941 340 700
Granon-Hostel	941 420 818
" - LaCasa Sonrises	687 877 891
Redecilla del Camino	947 580 283
Castildelgado	947 588 063
Victoria de La Rioja	947 585 220
Villamayor del Rio	947 580 566
Belorado- Santa Maria	947 580 085
Tostantos	947 580 371
Villambistia	680 501 887
Espinosa del Camino	678 479 361
Villafranca de Montes de Oca	947 582 124

San Juan de Ortega	947 560 438
Ages-San Rafael	947 430 392
Ages-Casa caracol	947 430 413
Ages-El Pajar	947 400 629
Atapuerca	661 580 882
Burgos-Centro	947 460 922
" -Divina Pastora	947 207 932
" -Youth Hostel	947 220 277
Tardajos	947 451 189
Rabe de los Calzadas	607 971 919
Hernillos Del Camino	947 411 050
Arroyo San Bol	628 927 317
Hontanas-El Bentido	947 378 597
" -Santa Brigida	628 927 317
Hontanas-San Juan	947 377 436
Castrojeriz	947 377 255
" - Casa Nostra	947 377 493
" -Centro	947 377 400
" -San Estaban	947 377 001
Itero de La Vega	979 151 822
" " -El Mochila	979 151 784
Boadilla del Camino	979 840 284
Fromista	979 811 089
Fromista-Estrella	979 810 053
Poblacion	979 811 099
" -Paso Camino	979 582 012
Villarmentero	662 279 102
" -Casona	979 065 978
Villalcazar	979 888 041
Carrion de los Condes	979 880 500
Calzadilla	979 883 187
Ledigos	979 883 605
Terradillos	979 883 679
Moratinos-Hostal	979 061 466
" -Albergue	979 061 465

San Nicolas	979 188 142
Rio Valderaduey	987 780 975
Sahagun-Clury	987 782 117
" -Monasterio	987 781 139
" -El Labriego	616 478 417
" -La Asturiana	987 780 073
" -Don Pacho	987 780 775
Sahagun-Escarcha	987 781 856
" -La Cordoniz	987 780 276
" -Alfonso VI	987 781 144
" -Puerta	987 781 880
Bercianos-Rivero	987 744 287
" -Parish	987 784 008
El Bergo Raneros-	
Domenico Laffi	987 330 023
" -El Nogal	627 229 331
" -El Perigrino	987 330 069
Calzada del Coto	987 781 233
Calzada de los Hermanillos	987 330 023
" -via Trajana	987 337 610
Reliegos-la Parada	987 317 880
" -Gaiferos	987 317 801
Mansilla	661 977 305
" -El Jardia	987 310 232
Villarente-El Delfin	987 312 065
" -San Pelayo	987 312 677
Adcahueja	987 205 896
Valdelafuente	987 218 134
Glorieta	987 081 832
" -Residensia	637 439 848
Leon- Monastery	987 252 866
Leon Hotels/Hostals	
Paris	987 238 600
LaPosada	987 213 173
Guzman	987 236 412

Leon	Hospoderia	987 213 173
	San Martin	987 875 187
	Boccalina	987 223 060
Cruce-Villa Paloma		987 300 990
" -San Froilan		987 223 060
Valverde		987 303 414
Villadangos		987 310 003
Villar de Mazarife		987 390 192
" -Casadejesus		686 053 390
" -Tio Pepe		987 390 517
Villarente-Santa Lucia		692 107 693
" -Molino Galochas		987 388 546
Hospital de Orbigo-Karl leisner		
		987 361 087
" -San Miguel		987 388 385
" -Verde		689 927 926
San Martin-Vieira		987 378 565
" -Santa Ana		987 378 653
" -San Martin		616 354 331
Villares de Orbigo		947 132 935
Santibanez		626 362 159
San Justo-Hostal		987 617 632
Astorga-Siervas de Maria		987 616 034
" -St Javier		987 618 532
" -Ecce Homo		620 960 060
Murias-Los Aquedas		636 067 840
" -Los Escuela		987 691 150
" -Casa Flor		609 478 323
Castrillo-Muni		655 803 706
" -Don Alvaro		987 053 990
Santa Catalina-El Caminante		987 691 098
" -Hospederia		987 691 411
" -Muni		987 691 819
El Ganso-Gabino		987 691 901
" -La Escuela		987 691 088

Puenta de Panote	650 952 721
Rabanal de Camino-Gaucelmo	987 691 901
" -del Pilar	987 631 621
" -Muni	987 631 687
Foncebadon-Convento	658 974 818
" -Monte Irego	695 452 950
" -La Cruz	665 258 169
Manjarin	No Phone
Acebo-Meson	987 695 074
-Taberna	No Phone
-Apostol Santiago	No Phone
-La Posada	987 057 875
-La Rosa	616 849 738
-La Trucha	987 695 548
-La Casa Del Monte	639 721 242
Riegodeambros	987 695 190
Molinaseca-Santa Marina	987 453 077
-San Rogue	987 453 077
Ponferrada-San Nicolas	987 413 381
" -Hotels	
El Castillo	987 456 227
La Encina	987 409 632
Los Temlaros	987 411 484
Numerous hotels on the other side of the river.	
Compostilla-Iglesia	987 424 441
Colambrianos	987 547 167
Villafranca-Muni	987 542 356
-Ave Feaix	987 540 229
-Vina Fermita	987 540 260
-de la Piedro	987 540 260
Pereje	987 540 138
" -Los Corinas	987 540 148

Trabadelo-Crispeta	620 329 386
" -Muni	647 635 831
La Portela de Valcarce	
" -Perigrino	987 543 197
" -Das Animas	619 048 626
" -Do Brasil	987 543 045
Vega de Valcarce-Muni	987 543 006
" -Magdalena	646 128 423
Ruitelan-Pequeno Potala	987 561 322
" -El Paradiso	987 684 137
Herrerias	654 353 940
" -Casa de Ferreiro	626 452 237
LaFaba	630 836 865
Laguna de Castilla	987 684 796
O'Cebreiro	660 396 809
Linares	982 367 166
Hospital de La Condesa	660 396 810
Alto de Polo	982 367 172
Fonfria-Casa nunez	982 161 335
" -Reboleira	982 181 271
Biduedo	982 187 299
Filloval	666 826 414
Triacastela-Garcia	982 548 024
" -Xunta	982 548 087
" -Oribio	982 548 085
" -Horta de Abel	608 080 556
" -Complexo	982 548 037
" -O'Novo	982 548 105
Pintin-Casa Cines	685 140 635
Calver	660 396 812
San Mamed	658 906 816
Samos-Monasterio	982 546 046
" -Albergue	982 546 087
" -Valde Samos	982 546 163

71

Vigo de Sarria		982 530 130
Sarria-Casa Poltre		606 226 067
"	-Mayor	685 148 474
"	-Xunta	660 396 813
"	-Durminento	982 531 099
"	- Internacional	982 535 109
"	-Los Blasones	600 512 565
"	-Dos Oito	629 461 770
"	-San Lazaro	982 530 626
"	-Monasterio	982 533 568
"	-Barbacoa	982 531 524
Ponte Aspera		982 531 934
Barbadelo-Xunta		660 396 814
"	-Pombal	686 718 732
"	-Casa de Carmen	982 532 294
Morgade		982 531 250
Ferreiros-Casa Cruceiro		982 541 240
"	-Xunta	686 744 940
Mercadoiro		982 545 359
Vilache		982 545 391
Portomarin-Mirador		982 545 323
"	-Ferramenteiro	982 545 362
"	-Xunta	982 545 143
"	-Caminante	982 545 176
"	-Ulteria	982545 067
"	-Porto Santiago	618 826 515
"	-Manuel	982 545 385
Gonzar-Xunta		982 157 840
"	-Casa Garcia	982 157 842
Castromaior		982 189 054
Hospital de la Cruz		982 545 232
Ventas-Casa Molar		696 794 507
"	-Cruceiro	658 064 917
Ligonde-Perigrino		687 550 527
"	-Escuela	679 816 061

Eirexe-Xunta	982 153 483
" -Meson	982 153 475
Calzada	982 183 744
Palas de Rei Pavillion-Xunta	607 481 536
" -Meson	636 834 065
Palas de Rei-Xunta	660 396 820
" -Buen Camino	982 380 233
San Xulian-Abrigadoiro	676 596 975
" -Casa Domingo	983 163 226
Cassanova-Xunta	982 173 483
" -Belboreta	609 124 717
O Coto-Somoza	981 507 372
" -Deutschen	981 507 337
Melide-Xunta	660 396 822
" -Apalpador	679 837 969
Boente Igrexa-Boente	981 501 874
" -Os Albergues	629 146 826
Casteneda-Albergue	981 501 711
" -La Calleja	605 787 382
Ribadiso-Xunta	981 501 185
" -Retiro Hostal	982 500 554
" -Don Quijote	981 500 139
" -Ulteria	981 500 471
" -Apostol	981 508 132
Arzua-Xunta	660 396 824
" -daFonte	659 999 496
" -Via Lactea	981 500 581
" -Los Caminantes	647 020 600
A Calzada	648 404 780
Salceda	981 502 767
Santa Irene-Xunta	660 396 825
" -Santa Irene	981 511 000

O Pedrouzo-Xunta	660 396 826
" -Porta	981 511 103
" -O Burgo	630 404 138
" -Edreira	981 511 365
" -Otero	671 663 374

Well Done !

Buen Camino

Camino Journal

Camino Journal

Camino Journal

Camino Journal

Camino Journal

Camino Journal

Camino Journal

Camino Journal

Camino Journal

Camino Journal

Camino Journal

Camino Journal

Camino Journal

Camino Journal

Camino Journal

Camino Journal

Camino Journal

Camino Journal

Camino Journal

Camino Journal

Camino Journal

Camino Journal

Camino Journal

Camino Journal

Camino Journal

Camino Journal

Camino Journal

Camino Journal

Camino Journal

Camino Journal

Camino Journal

Camino Journal

Camino Journal

Camino Journal

Camino Journal

Camino Journal

Camino Journal

Manufactured by Amazon.ca
Bolton, ON

45464415R00063